P9-DUE-169

Empire State Building

MIKAYA PRESS

NEW YORK

Author Acknowledgments

Thanks to John Tauranac, author of *The Empire State Building:
The Making of a Landmark*, for his careful reading and rereading of the text.
Thanks to consulting engineer Donald Friedman for casting a rigorous
eye over the details of engineering and construction.
Their suggestions have been invaluable.
Errors of fact or interpretation are mine alone.

—E.M.

Editor: Stuart Waldman
Design: Lesley Ehlers Design

Other Books by Elizabeth Mann
The Brooklyn Bridge
The Great Pyramid
The Great Wall
The Roman Colosseum
The Panama Canal
Machu Picchu
Hoover Dam
Tikal

Copyright © 2003 Mikaya Press
Original Illustrations copyright © Alan Witschonke
Photograph page 42-43 copyright © Jay Maisel
All rights reserved. Published by Mikaya Press Inc.
Wonders of the World Books is a registered trademark of Mikaya Press Inc.
No part of this publication may be reproduced in whole or in part or stored in a retrieval system,
or transmitted in any form or by any means, electronic, mechanical,
photocopying,recording or otherwise, without written permission of the publisher.
For information regarding permission, write to: Mikaya Press Inc.,
12 Bedford Street, New York, N.Y.10014. Distributed in North America by:
Firefly Books Ltd., 3680 Victoria Park Ave., Willowdale, Ontario, M2H3KI

Cataloging-in-Publication Data Available from the Library of Congress

Empire State Building

A WONDERS OF THE WORLD BOOK

BY ELIZABETH MANN

WITH ILLUSTRATIONS BY ALAN WITSCHONKE

MIKAYA PRESS

NEW YORK

On October 1, 1929, Alfred E. Smith joked with the reporters gathered on the roof of the Waldorf-Astoria Hotel at the corner of 34th Street and Fifth Avenue in New York City. He grinned for the cameras, and he and John J. Raskob tugged on a rope that was tied to a section of stone railing. The elaborately carved piece, loosened earlier by workmen, broke free easily and fell with a crash. Cameras clicked and the crowd applauded. The carefully staged ceremony officially began the demolition of the Waldorf-Astoria. When the hotel was gone, the world's tallest building would rise in its place.

For Smith and Raskob the event marked the end of an uncertain time. The year before, after four terms as governor of New York State, Smith had run for president of the United States. He was soundly defeated by Herbert Hoover. Afterwards he was low on money and badly in need of a job. At around the same time, Raskob had lost his job as vice president of carmaker General Motors. Money was not a concern for him—he had made a considerable fortune by investing in the stock market—but he had to figure out how he would spend his time, and his millions of dollars, in the years to come.

No one knows exactly what happened next. Some say Raskob approached Smith with the idea in a men's room in New York City. Some say Smith brought it up on a golf course during a Florida vacation. Whatever happened, the two friends became partners. Even though neither of them had any experience in construction or architecture, they decided to build the Empire State Building. Always the energetic and friendly politician, Smith was to be the official boss of the project, meeting with the press and the public, as well as with architects and engineers. Raskob, a private businessman, chose to work behind the scenes, persuading wealthy friends to invest in the building with him.

On August 29, 1929, the front page of *The New York Times* announced, "Smith to Help Build Highest Skyscraper."

The rooftop demolition ceremony was one of many events that Al Smith, wearing his trademark brown derby hat, staged for the press. It was part of his job to draw attention to the Empire State Building. Unlike his partner, John Raskob, Smith loved being in the spotlight.

The Empire State Building was not the first skyscraper—far from it. Skyscrapers appeared in America in the 1800s. They came about because of a great change that was sweeping the country: industrialization. Manufacturing expanded so rapidly during the 19th century that it became more important than agriculture. As a result, many people left their farms and moved into cities to work in factories and offices.

At the same time, European immigrants were traveling to American cities to take advantage of the job opportunities there. As millions of workers arrived, new and bigger buildings were required, but cities like New York and Chicago were already crowded. There wasn't enough land for sprawling factories and big office buildings. Taller buildings with more floors would have provided more useful space on the same amount of land, but height was limited. The materials and methods available for construction at the time were not practical or safe for a tall building.

Bearing-wall construction was the most common way of building in American cities in the 19th century. It was called that because the walls carried the weight of the entire building and everything in it. Bearing walls were made of stone or brick, and they needed to be thick in order to be strong. The taller the building, the heavier it was and the greater the weight the walls had to bear. Greater weight required thicker walls, especially on the lower stories where the weight was greatest.

A tall bearing-wall building wasn't practical. The thick walls took up valuable floor space. The windows had to be small, so less sunlight reached the rooms inside. Nineteenth-century bearing-wall buildings were rarely more than six stories tall.

BEARING-WALL CONSTRUCTION
❶ A bearing wall rises brick by brick, row by row.
❷ Openings are left for windows, but they cannot be too large because openings weaken a brick wall.
❸ Beams are built into the bearing walls.
❹ Floors are laid on top of the beams.
❺ The beams carry the weight of floors, furniture, and people to the bearing walls.
❻ The walls are thicker at the bottom of the building because they bear the weight of the entire building.

The population continued to grow in America's cities, and so did the need for taller buildings. Fortunately the 19th century was an exciting time of innovation. Inventors, engineers, and builders experimented with new construction ideas and made improvements on old ones.

In 1849 an iron manufacturer named James Bogardus built a factory in which a metal framework, instead of bearing walls, carried the weight of the building. The framework supported the building from the inside, the way a skeleton supports a human body. The walls, like human skin, carried no weight at all. They were called "curtain walls" because they were attached to the framework and hung from it like curtains.

A metal framework could be strong without taking up space. The windows in a curtain wall could be large enough to flood the rooms with light. That meant that a framework building could be tall without giving up space and light.

FRAMEWORK CONSTRUCTION

❶ The metal framework is constructed first.

❷ The curtain wall and windows are attached to the framework.

❸ The weight of the building—the curtain walls as well as the floors, furniture, and people—is carried by the metal framework.

Framework construction was an improvement, but a framework is only as strong as the metal it is made of. Cast iron was the strongest metal available when Bogardus built his factory. At best it could only support a building 16 stories tall. Something stronger was needed if buildings were to climb higher.

In 1859, Henry Bessemer invented a way to make steel, a metal five times stronger than iron. Years of improvements followed, and in the 1870s the Roebling family used the new metal on the Brooklyn Bridge. It was the first time that steel had been used for construction, and it was a complete success. Other builders took notice.

In 1885, two years after the Brooklyn Bridge was completed, architect William LeBaron Jenney used steel in the framework of a building in Chicago. The newspapers of the time called it a "cloudscraper"—the word "skyscraper" didn't come into use until 1889. Though it was only ten stories tall, Jenney's building is known as the first real skyscraper because of the steel in the framework. Following Jenney's lead, more builders used steel in framework construction, and buildings grew taller.

Tall buildings presented another problem that had to be solved. A 10-story building wasn't much use if people couldn't get to the upper floors. In the 19th century, elevators were used mainly for lifting freight. Elevator cables broke so often that people preferred to take the stairs.

In 1853 Elisha Graves Otis invented the automatic elevator brake. If a cable broke, his invention automatically stopped the elevator and kept it from crashing to the ground. After years of improvements, the first passenger elevator to be powered by electricity and equipped with an automatic safety brake was installed in a building in New York in 1889. From then on, no matter how high the building, the top floor could be reached as easily and safely as the lobby.

With steel to support them and elevators to climb them, buildings could reach for the skies, and they did. A skyscraper boom swept the country. By 1929, in New York City alone, there were 188 buildings that were over 20 stories tall!

Two rare photos of the southern end of Manhattan, both taken from the same spot in Brooklyn, show how dramatically the skyscraper boom changed the New York City skyline. In 1890, there is only one tall structure, a church steeple.

In 1921, barely 30 years later, the skyline is already transformed. The church steeple is hidden behind a wall of new skyscrapers.

In 1929 the Chrysler Building wasn't finished, but the spire was in place.

The growth of manufacturing and population in American cities created a need for skyscrapers. New inventions made it possible to build them. And there was another force driving the skyscraper boom.

As manufacturing expanded, people like John Raskob became very rich. These new multimillionaires were proud of their accomplishments and they enjoyed showing off their wealth. They spent extravagantly on everything from automobiles to artwork, but there was no better way to display wealth than to build a skyscraper that towered over a city.

If being the envy of a city wasn't enough of a reason for a millionaire to build a fantastic skyscraper, there was also a practical reason. Tenants were willing to pay higher rents in tall buildings. Naturally the owner of the tallest one collected the highest rents and became even wealthier. In New York City the competition to see who could build the biggest skyscraper became a hotly contested race.

In August of 1929 the Chrysler Building on 42nd Street seemed a likely winner. It was 61 stories tall and still climbing, but no one knew how tall it would be. The owner, car manufacturer Walter Chrysler, thought secrecy would give him an advantage in the skyscraper race. He would not reveal his plans.

Smith and Raskob had no way of knowing what Chrysler had in mind, but they took a chance. They announced that the Empire State Building would be 1,000 feet tall. They hoped that would make their building the tallest.

When Chrysler heard the news, he acted immediately. Secretly, inside the topmost floors of his building, a thin metal spire was quickly constructed. In October it was hoisted up through the top of the building and attached. In just 90 minutes, the Chrysler Building shot from 925 to 1,048 feet tall.

Raskob and Smith would not be outdone. They worked closely with the architects, Shreve, Lamb and Harmon, and the builders, Starrett Brothers and Eken, to figure out a way to add more height.

In November Al Smith made another announcement. Five more stories would be added to the Empire State Building, making it 1,050 feet tall, two feet taller than the tip of the Chrysler Building spire. It was too late for Walter Chrysler to add anything more. Smith and Raskob had won the skyscraper race before the first beam was in place.

Reporters weren't the only ones who were intrigued by Al Smith's plans for the mooring mast. Artists did fanciful paintings, like the one on this postcard, of airships docking at the Empire State Building.

Still they weren't satisfied. Two feet was too small a lead for them. To make their building even taller, and to attract more attention to it, Smith and Raskob decided to add a very unusual tower to the top.

During the 1920s people had become enchanted with the idea of air travel. At the time, passenger airplane flights to Europe still seemed impossible. Instead the dream was that passengers would be carried back and forth over the Atlantic by lighter-than-air dirigibles. It was thought to be the latest in modern travel, as luxurious as an ocean liner, and twice as fast. Smith and Raskob wanted to take advantage of this exciting new development. Their unusual tower was to be a mooring mast, the only one of its kind, a dock for dirigibles high above New York City!

Al Smith delighted in talking about it. He described the huge airships arriving from Paris and tying fast to the mooring mast. He described passengers disembarking from the dirigible cabin and stepping, luggage and all, onto the sidewalks of Manhattan just seven minutes later. His accounts were vivid and his excitement was contagious. Eager newspaper reporters were only too happy to print his stories. Smith's boundless enthusiasm for the mooring mast helped keep the Empire State Building constantly in the news.

The Waldorf-Astoria Hotel was the last word in luxury and elegance when it opened in 1893, but people's tastes changed. By the end of the 1920s, it had begun to seem old-fashioned.

While Smith, Raskob, the architects, and the engineers labored over plans and drawings in the race for height, workers at the construction site were competing in a different, equally frantic race. They were racing against time.

Smith and Raskob wanted their building to be finished as fast as possible, and for a very practical reason. The sooner construction was finished, the sooner tenants could move in and begin paying rent.

Starrett Brothers and Eken kept 600 workers busy with crowbars and sledgehammers tearing down the Waldorf-Astoria. It was not an easy task. The magnificent hotel had been built to last, and it was as sturdy as the day it opened. Even with crews on the job day and night, demolition took five months!

Excavation of the foundation hole began before demolition was even finished. Like all massive structures, the Empire State Building had to rest on a firm foundation. The bedrock below the site was a dense, solid stone called Manhattan schist. It was the perfect base for the giant building, but it was not easy to break apart. Workers resorted to dynamite to carve the foundation hole into the bedrock.

Engines roared as trucks strained to haul their heavy loads of debris up ramps to the street. The workers in Egypt who pulled giant stone blocks up similar ramps to build the Great Pyramid were probably slower, but they would certainly have been quieter.

Blasting with explosives in the center of a city of seven million people had to be done very carefully. Cars and pedestrians jammed the busy streets around the work site. To protect them from flying chunks of stone, heavy mats of woven steel were heaped on the bedrock before each blast. The mats also helped muffle the noise of the explosions, a welcome relief for people in the neighborhood.

Unfortunately, nothing could be done to muffle the sounds of steam shovels, trucks, drills, and jack hammers. Neighbors had to endure months of deafening clamor.

During demolition and excavation, trucks filled with rubble and stone rumbled heavily through the streets of Manhattan, making a total of 28,529 trips. The debris was loaded onto barges in the East River and dumped in the Atlantic Ocean 20 miles from shore.

On April 7, 1930, a forest of 210 giant steel columns began to sprout. The columns rested on concrete bases, called piers, that were sunk deep into the bedrock.

The first level of columns in the foundation hole were the most massive in the building. They had to be—they carried the full weight of the building. Each one stood nearly 16 feet tall and weighed 44 tons. When the building was finished, each column would support 5,000 tons of skyscraper!

Hundreds of horizontal steel beams were attached to the columns, joining them together in a three-dimensional grid. The beams didn't have to be as massive as the columns. They contributed to the strength of the framework, but they didn't carry as much weight.

Concrete was used for the floors because it made a strong, smooth surface. It also protected the beams from fire. This was very important in a skyscraper. Steel could not burn but, without fireproofing, heat from a fire could soften it enough to weaken the framework and endanger the entire building.

DOWN IN THE FOUNDATION HOLE

❶ Pier holes—210 of them—were blasted deep into the bedrock

❷ Piers were created by pouring concrete into the pier holes. Pieces of steel embedded in the wet concrete served as anchors for the columns.

❸ Each steel column was lowered onto its pier by crane and attached to the protruding steel anchors.

❹ Steel beams were attached to the columns.

❺ Concrete floors were supported by the beams.

Columns, beams, concrete floor. Columns, beams, concrete floor. The steps were repeated story after story.

The steelworkers set the pace for the rest of the construction. Everything depended on them, and they outdid themselves. The framework rose at the record-breaking rate of four and a half stories a week.

Steelworkers were the superheroes on the job. They performed amazing acts of skill and daring on a stage that could be seen for miles in every direction.

Photographer Lewis Hine followed the steelworkers to the highest reaches of the framework to capture them on the job. He took some of his shots from the end of a crane cable that suspended him in the air nearly a quarter of a mile above the ground.

These workers are perched on the mooring mast framework.

It was against safety regulations, and common sense, to "ride the ball," but some workers couldn't resist. The worker in this photo is higher than the top of the Chrysler Building behind him.

A steelworker enjoys a stupendous view of the city during a break.

Hine named this photo "Icarus," after the bold character in Greek myth who flew too close to the sun and crashed to the earth. No matter how high he went, Hine's Icarus always made it safely back down to the ground. Beyond him the Hudson River and New Jersey can be seen.

A beam, with a steelworker on board, dangles from a crane cable. Two levelers guide the steel into position while clinging to a column. The southern end of Manhattan stretches out behind them.

Each giant piece of steel bobbed and swayed delicately at the end of a steel cable as a crane lifted it through the air. "Levelers" pushed and tugged at the massive beam, easing it into position. They lined up the holes in the beam with those in the column, getting ready for the riveting crew.

A top-notch riveting crew was thrilling to watch. Graceful as dancers, the men moved about on narrow steel beams and wooden planks doing jobs high in the air that would have been difficult even with both feet on solid ground.

Each crew had four members. The "heater" kept a coal fire blazing in a small furnace and heated the mushroom-shaped steel rivets until they were softened and glowing bright red. Using tongs, he snatched a hot rivet from the coals and tossed it to the "catcher." Sometimes the toss had to be as long as 75 feet. The catcher caught the flying rivet in a bucket, grabbed it with tongs, and slipped the thin end through the holes in the steel pieces that were to be joined together. The "bucker-up" pressed a tool called a "dolly bar" against the round head of the rivet with all his strength, while the "riveter" turned on his air hammer and held it against the stem end. The powerful hammer slammed twice a second against the stem end, mashing the still-soft steel into a mushroom shape. As the rivet cooled and hardened, it fused with the steel around it, locking the beams and columns together permanently. Long before it had cooled, another red-hot rivet had sailed up to the catcher and was being hammered by the riveter.

Some of the best crews, the ones that could place a rivet a minute, came from northern New York State and Canada. They were Mohawks from the Akwasasne and Kahnawake tribes. Since the 1890s, they had been "booming out"—traveling the country to work on the high steel of bridges and skyscrapers. Their balance, skill, and apparent lack of fear were legendary. For the Mohawk, steelworking was more than just a job. It had become a part of their tribal tradition. Boys learned the trade from their fathers, and tools were handed down reverently from one generation to the next.

Toss, catch, insert, rivet. Toss, catch, insert, rivet. Over and over, with split-second timing, the crews repeated the steps. Their moves were as precisely synchronized as a trapeze act. They had to be—the crew members depended on each other for their lives.

When work began on the curtain wall, more steps were added to the construction process.

The curtain wall was important to Smith and Raskob. It was the outside of the building—it would be seen from streets and parks, from neighboring states, even from ships at sea. They wanted it to be spectacular.

Shreve, Lamb and Harmon came up with a sleek, modern design that used pale Indiana limestone, shiny nickel-steel strips (mullions), and aluminum panels (spandrels). It was beautiful enough to please Smith and Raskob and practical enough to please Starrett Brothers and Eken.

The architects' design allowed Starrett Brothers and Eken to save precious time on the job. The large pieces of stone and metal arrived ready to install. All the workers had to do was put them in place and attach them to the framework.

The tall, silvery mullions were attached first. Then the aluminum spandrels, each etched with a lovely angular design, and the slabs of limestone were slid into position behind them. The red-framed windows sat atop the spandrels. The mullions concealed the rough edges of the limestone, the spandrels, and the windows, so workers didn't have to spend time smoothing and polishing them.

Behind the curtain wall was an inner wall of brick that would help keep the building warm and fireproof. When construction was finished, the brick wall would be sandwiched between the curtain wall and the office walls inside the building. The bricks would be hidden, so bricklayers did not have to concern themselves with doing tidy work. They could move at lightning speed.

Assembling a curtain wall out of ready-made sections that didn't need to be smoothed and polished helped Starrett Brothers and Eken in the race against time. It was one of many time-saving innovations invented on the Empire State Building.

Mullions, spandrels, slabs, windows, bricks. Mullions, spandrels, slabs, windows, bricks. The steps were repeated over and over by the workers who swarmed up the building just a few stories behind the riveting crews. The bricklayers worked safely inside the building. Curtain-wall workers stood on wooden scaffolds that hung high above the honking cars and rushing pedestrians in the streets below.

❶ Nickel-steel mullion
❷ Aluminum spandrel
❸ Limestone slab
❹ Window
❺ Brick wall

As the framework and curtain wall climbed, the inside of the building came alive also. Carpenters built walls, plumbers installed sinks, and electricians connected lights. Painters, plasterers, and tilesetters worked their magic, turning rough concrete, wood, and brick into bright, airy offices. The Otis Elevator Company installed 67 of the fastest passenger elevators ever made and painstakingly tested them. August of 1930 was the busiest month. There were 3,500 workers on the site every day doing 60 different kinds of jobs.

As always, Starrett Brothers and Eken found ways to make the work go faster. They salvaged elevators from the old Waldorf-Astoria and used them to hoist supplies. Doorknobs, toilets, radiators, light switches, and a thousand other items were whisked upward in elevators that had once carried ladies in silk dresses to afternoon tea.

Using hoists in this way was a new idea in construction. It was faster and safer than using cranes. (Steel still had to be lifted by crane—the pieces were too big to fit in an elevator car.)

Materials were unloaded from the hoists and onto little railroad cars. The cars were pushed by hand along miniature railroad tracks to the workers who needed the supplies. As work was finished on each story, the tracks were taken apart and re-installed on a higher floor.

Like the supply hoists, the little railroads were another clever innovation that Starrett Brothers and Eken devised to save precious construction time.

It hardly seems possible that this rough construction hoist was once an elegant Waldorf-Astoria elevator car.

The railroad cars were small, but the loads were heavy. Two workers are needed to push this load of limestone slabs to the curtain-wall workers.

Diagonal pieces of steel, like the one here, braced the framework against heavy winds. The worker in this picture has wrapped the windbrace in wire mesh and is coating it with concrete to protect it from fire.

Two strong workers struggle to move a full load of terra cotta tiles along the tracks. Terra cotta was used for walls inside the building because it was fireproof.

Safety was not sacrificed for speed on the Empire State Building. Much had been learned about safety during the skyscraper boom, and Starrett Brothers and Eken used that knowledge well. They knew that workers who were exhausted, thirsty, or hungry were more likely to be careless and have accidents. They planned the work schedule to prevent accidents.

Eight-hour days, five-day weeks, and half-hour lunch breaks all contributed to the workers' well-being. Young water carriers brought cool drinks to everyone on the job, and cafeterias on five different floors sold quick, inexpensive lunches. A 50-person safety crew roamed the building. Their only job: to spot unsafe conditions and immediately correct them. A nurse was on the site at all times, just in case, and a doctor visited daily.

Construction in the 1930s was a hazardous occupation, and even the best precautions couldn't prevent all accidents. In the end, six workers lost their lives on the Empire State Building. Despite the dangers of their job, none of those who died were steelworkers.

Even the inspectors occasionally found themselves in risky situations.

Workers on the Empire State Building enjoyed good pay as well as safe working conditions. A riveter, for example, could earn $15 a day, a princely sum at that time. This comfortable situation was not destined to last. When their jobs on the building ended, many workers would not see another paycheck for a long time. America had changed since the building began, and the change was not good.

On October 29, 1929, less than a month after Al Smith's demolition ceremony, the New York Stock Market on Wall Street had "crashed." Businesses that had once been worth millions of dollars became worthless overnight. It was the beginning of an economic depression.

During a depression, companies go out of business and workers lose their jobs. Banks close and families lose their life savings. There had been other depressions in America, but this one, the Great Depression, was the worst ever.

By the fall of 1930, a quarter of American workers were unemployed. The weather grew colder, and people couldn't afford coal to heat their homes. Al Smith had grown up in the slums of Manhattan at the foot of the Brooklyn Bridge. He knew firsthand what it was like to be cold during a New York City winter. He did what he could. He had workers cut discarded lumber into coal stove-size pieces and haul it to a nearby vacant lot. It was free for the taking, and many New Yorkers relied on Al Smith's firewood for heat that winter.

Construction projects all over the city were closing down, but work on the Empire State Building never slowed. John Raskob used his unusual skill in business to protect his investment in the building from the Great Depression.

The Empire State Building rose at a dizzying rate.

The workers were able to maintain their fantastic speed because they always had materials to work with. Starrett Brothers and Eken left nothing to chance. A seemingly endless stream of trucks poured onto the construction site according to a precise schedule. Everything from Pennsylvania steel to Indiana limestone to German marble had to arrive exactly when it was needed.

Starrett Brothers and Eken set a record for speed on the Empire State Building that is not likely to be broken. Weekly photographs of the job site show how quickly the building climbed.

April 1930

The first columns and beams are placed in the foundation hole.

August 1930

There are 3,500 workers on the job, more than during any other month.

May 1930

Thirteen stories of steel framework are in place.

June 1930

The framework reaches the 25th story and the curtain wall is not far behind.

July 1930

The framework jumps to the 37th story. Work inside the building speeds up.

September 1930

On September 22, the framework reaches the 86th floor two weeks ahead of schedule. Workers raise an American flag from the top to celebrate.

November 1930

The mooring mast framework is completed. Al Smith, though terrified at being 102 stories above the ground, places the last rivet. It is made of solid gold.

March 1931

The exterior of the building is finished, but work continues on the inside.

The finished skyscraper was everything Smith and Raskob had hoped it would be—beautiful, modern, and very tall. Unfortunately it was nearly empty. The Great Depression had caught up with the Empire State Building. There were no tenants for the handsome new offices. Reporters who had once cheered the world's tallest skyscraper nicknamed it the "Empty State Building." Al Smith, always hopeful, kept the lights on at night so that the building at least looked occupied.

In September of 1931, plans were made to test the mooring mast by having a dirigible dock at the mast and deliver a bundle of newspapers, hot off the presses, to the top of the Empire State Building.

The experiment was also a publicity stunt, so Al Smith assembled a small crowd on the open deck of the 102nd floor for the occasion. He clutched his brown derby hat to his head as the wind pushed and tugged at the approaching airship. The pilot struggled to steady it. Docking was out of the question, but he thought he could still deliver the papers. A worker reached again and again for the dangling rope that held the bundle. "Hold my legs, somebody, in case I get pulled!" he said, and with John Raskob, one of the wealthiest men in the world, clinging to his trousers, the worker finally grabbed the rope, cut it, and handed the bundle of papers to Smith.

Even Al Smith had to agree that the experiment had been a failure. The constant, unpredictable city winds were too dangerous. The first airship delivery to the Empire State Building was also the last. Dirigible docking was quietly abandoned.

Offices were empty and the mooring mast was unused, but the Empire State Building came to life in unexpected ways. The colorful marble lobby was busy every day from early morning until late at night. Nearly a million people passed through it during the first year the building was open. A dollar bought a ride in a swift, wood-paneled elevator that ended less than a minute later at the viewing deck on the 86th floor. The knee-weakening view of New York City was like nothing ever seen before.

The Empire State Building was a hopeful sight for New Yorkers who watched it climb like a rocket from a hole in the ground during the Great Depression. When it was completed, it continued to lift their spirits. It had not been defeated by the Depression, and neither would the city. Whether they were gazing up at it from the streets or looking out from its observation deck, people fell in love with the handsome skyscraper. It soon became New York's most famous landmark, recognized all over the world.

The Empire State Building topped off New York's skyscraper boom. During the 40 years before it was built, the record for the tallest building was broken over and over. For 40 years after it was finished, nothing came close. The Empire State Building remained the tallest in the world until 1972 when the first tower of the World Trade Center was completed.

In 1981, at 50 years of age, the Empire State Building was declared to be a New York City Landmark. It can never be torn down or changed in any way. It will continue to be the same striking exclamation point in the city skyline that it was in 1931.

The Empire State Building Through the Years

The Empire State Building opened on May 1, 1931. Al Smith included his grandchildren in the ceremony. He moved into an office on the 32nd floor, where he worked tirelessly to attract tenants to the building. By the time of his death in 1944, he had the satisfaction of knowing that his efforts had paid off. The building was well on the way to being fully rented.

The Empire State Building has appeared in over 100 movies, but the best known is still *King Kong*, which was made in 1933.

On a Saturday morning in July of 1945, a military bomber, lost in the fog, crashed into the 79th floor of the building. Fourteen people were killed in the crash and the fire that followed, but the building stood firm. The fireproofing worked; the steel framework was not weakened. The building was open for business as usual when workers arrived on Monday morning.

In 1950 the mooring mast stopped being an embarrassing reminder of a bad idea. A new industry, television, used it as the base for a 222-foot-tall broadcast antenna. A children's program called *The Howdy Doody Show* was broadcast from it to television screens in living rooms over 50 miles away, and people's lives were changed forever. The antenna is still used today.

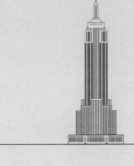

Facts

Height at the 86th floor—1,050 feet

Height at the top of the mooring mast—1,250 feet

Height at the top of the television antenna—1,472 feet

Area of the ground floor—83,890 square feet

Area at the 30th-floor setback—24,924 square feet

Number of elevators—64

Number of Windows—6,500

Time required for demolition of Waldorf-Astoria—5 months

Time required for raising steel to 86th floor—6 months

Time from demolition ceremony to opening ceremony—19 months

Most workers on the job at one time—3,500

Workers killed on the job—6

Viewing deck visitors in first year after opening—nearly 1,000,000

Annual visitors now—over 2,000,000

Glossary

Beams— horizontal steel pieces

Columns— vertical steel pieces

Hoist— an elevator used during construction

Mullions— vertical strips of nickel-steel used in the curtain wall

Piers— concrete supports under the columns that transferred the weight of the building from the columns to the bedrock

Setback— moving the walls of a building back from the edge of the building site to reduce the area of the building and make it narrower

Skyscraper— a building over 20 stories tall that is supported by an internal steel framework

Spandrels— pieces of cast aluminum used in the curtain wall

Steel— a metal made from iron that is five times stronger than iron

Note: Words used in architecture and construction often have more than one meaning. The words are defined here as they are used in this book.

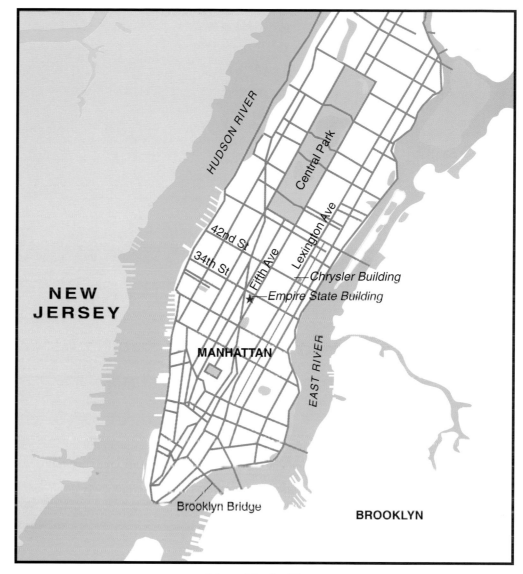

New York City

Index

Selected Bibliography

Architectural Forum, "The Empire State Building, I-XI," a series of 11 articles by various authors, January 1930-May 1931.

Gayle, Margot and Carol Gayle, *Cast-Iron Architecture in America: The Significance of James Bogardus,* New York:: W. W. Norton & Company, 1998.

Goldman, Jonathan, *The Empire State Building Book,* New York: St. Martin's Press, 1980.

Hill, Richard, *Skywalkers: A History of Indian Ironworkers, Brantford, Ont.:* Woodland Indian Cultural Centre, 1987.

Hine, Lewis, *The Empire State Building,* New York: Prestel USA, 1998.

Mitchell, Joseph, "The Mohawks in High Steel," *The New Yorker,* September 17, 1949.

The New York Times, various articles, August, 1929-September, 1931.

Pacelle, Mitchell, *Empire: A Tale of Obsession, Betrayal, and the Battle for an American Icon,* New York: John Wiley & Sons, 2001.

Shreve, R. H., "The Empire State Building Organization," *The Architectural Forum,* June, 1930.

Starrett, W. A., *Skyscrapers and the Men Who Build Them,* New YorkL Charles Scribner's Sons, 1928.

Tauranac, John, *The Empire State: The Making of a Landmark,* New York: St. Martin's Griffin, 1995.

Whiffen, Marcus and Frederic Koeper, *American Architecture 1607-1976,* Cambridge: The M.I.T Press, 1981.

Willis, Carol, ed., *Building the Empire State,* New York: W. W. Norton & Company, Inc., 1998.

Credits

Page 11: Museum of the City of New York.
Page 12: CORBIS
Page 13: Collection of Ronette Riley.
Page 14-15: Avery Architectural and Fine Arts Library, Columbia University in the City of New York.
Page 18-20: Avery Architectural and Fine Arts Library, Columbia University in the City of New York.
Page 26-27: The Skyscraper Museum.
Page 28: Avery Architectural and Fine Arts Library, Columbia University in the City of New York.
Page 32-33: Avery Architectural and Fine Arts Library, Columbia University in the City of New York.
Page 42-43: Jay Maisel Photography.
Page 44-45: CORBIS
Page 45 (bottom center): Ernie Sisto/*The New York Times.*

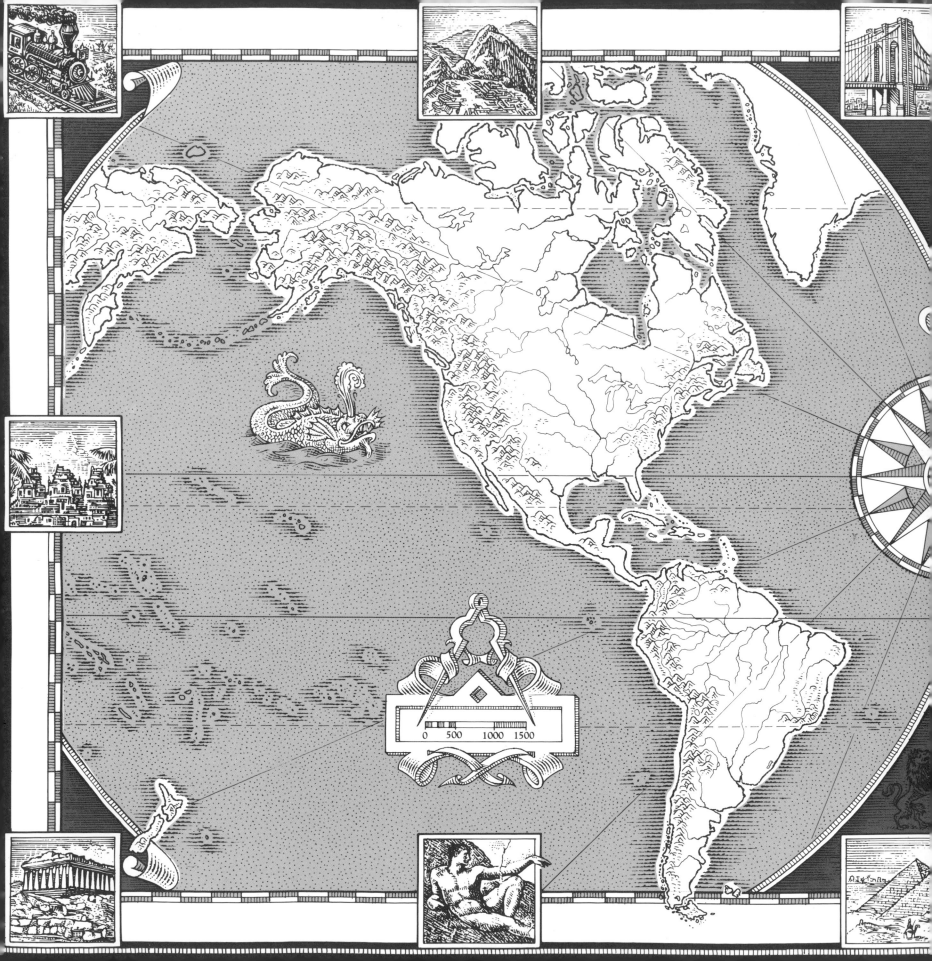